THE NOTES

Laura Shenton

THE NOTES

Laura Shenton

Iridescent Toad Publishing

Iridescent Toad Publishing.

©Laura Shenton 2024
All rights reserved.

Laura Shenton asserts the moral right to be identified as the author of this work.

No part of this publication may be reproduced, stored or transmitted in any form or by any means, electronic, mechanical, photocopying, recording, scanning, or otherwise without written permission from the publisher. It is illegal to copy this book, post it to a website, or distribute it by any other means without permission.

All cover images used under a commercial license.

First edition. ISBN: 978-1-913779-96-2

A soaring melody
Or a pounding bass
It can't help but bring
A smile to your face

Your mind, it wanders
Your soul, it flies
Let your ears take this
And not your eyes

What's that song called?
Will I hear it again?

To meet only once
Sets a slight pang of pain

Songs in your head
When you're resting in bed

The mood will take you
Where you need to go

Pulsing rhythms
Dictating your mind

A train of thought
Chugga-chugga-chugga

Shall I listen to that song
That I've got in mind?
Or sit back and see
What my brain may find?

Music in my head
Music in my bed

Music in the pub
As my mates and I laugh

Music when I'm lonely
Lonely in the soul

Thank you, music
You're everywhere

As soon as the needle
Goes down on the record

Something important
Is about to happen

Press play
No regrets

No regrets

When you find a new song
By a favourite band

That's exciting

When you find a new song
By a band unknown

Wow! Let the journey begin

When a favourite song
Comes on at a party

It lifts the mood
Higher and higher

Earphones are on
Don't talk to me

Tunes coming through
Need melodies in me

Disco, punk, rave
Metal, thrash, new wave

Give me the tunes
Come on, make my day

Closing my eyes
Need my mind somewhere else

A haunting symphony
Will take me away

Vocals or an instrumental

Either way
Emotions hit hard

And just when you think
You've had enough

You hear something wonderful
Ah, that's the stuff

Music in the shops
Background top pops

Music in the home
Unplug the phone

The music is busy
The music is hectic

But calm on the sofa
With pets on your lap
You're calm in your bubble
You're not feeling crap

Even the quietest volume
Can make the biggest impact

Aggressive violins
And timpani to punctuate

The music is so angry
Beethoven in a two and eight

Cocktail party
Mocktail party

Tinkling piano in the background
Give me some of that

Just twelve notes in western music
So much has been done with them

It's mindblowing

Life is surely too short
When nobody ever
Can hear all the music
No matter how clever

Music is big
Music is broad
And much of it lives
Not pressing record

Even the worst singer
Has something to say
Something to express

Let them sing

Music can save

What a wonderful distraction
From what's hard in this world

Everyone's life has a soundtrack

Musical memory

Events carried
Through the essence of melody

Every instrument
A different timbre

So much potential
So much scope

When the pitch bends
On an old and loved cassette...

There's something endearing about that

Music is a safe place
To feel

Each and every emotion
Come one, come all

Music from the heart
Music from the soul

Music for the heart
Music for the soul

Perhaps you haven't heard
Your favourite song yet

So much that is new
Could fall through the net

Music goosebumps
What a feeling

Spine-tingling
Rare-yet-addictive
Music goosebumps

Instrument and voice combine
Creating beauty, so divine
Music is a constant friend
As part of life, a welcome blend

Music magic
Music art
Those soundwaves
Play a vital part

Music speaks to the heart
A language that never falls apart
Bringing the joy, soothing the pain
Music, an all-round good refrain

Transcending time
Transcending space
Music for the human race

Rhythm and melody
Magic entwined
Helping the day
Feel good and fine

Music paints pictures
Deep in our mind
Abundant with colours
And textures in kind

A landscape of sound
And sweet harmony
Peace in escapism
That is the key

From quiet whispers
To boisterous cries
From raging anger
To blissful sighs

The sound of the keys, soft and slow
Or fast and furious, in frantic flow

A flurry of sound at every stroke
Such emotion can a piano evoke

Strummed with love, a melody starts

From gentle meanderings to fiery riffs
With every chord, a story unfolds

Gentle guitar
Powerful guitar

Forever to reign

From the hills to the sea
Five notes

Sweet pentatonic scale
Flowing free

A tapestry of sound
Such layers to be found
An orchestra
Is thus profound

Misheard the lyrics?
Heard them, but didn't understand them?

Never mind

As long as you enjoyed it, that's what matters

Besides, there's always next time

The trumpet makes
A wonderful toot
Blasting sound
Its glorious fruit

Dark and heavy
Or sparkly bubblegum
May your music match
Your mood for the day

The catharsis
In the song
That pleads the cry
For help

Nobody alone

So many notes
In just one song

Placed with purpose
Or by coincidence

They all contribute

Jazz

A rhythm that makes you lose control

With every beat, it comes alive
Making you want to dance and jive

A mixture of blues, swing, and funk
Leaving all your troubles sunk

You can feel the beat
It's contagious

Go and dance
It's not outrageous

A good rhythm never fails to please
Making you nod your head with ease

The jukebox
A tomb of musical gold
With classics
That will never grow old

Trippy music
Full of flair
From times
Of psychedelic fayre

From lazy jams
To soulful cries
A solo grabs you
Makes you fly

A sound of dreams
So many themes
Ideas bursting
At the seams

Music on the radio
A blast from the past

A memory jogged, a feeling stirred
Long may it last

From deep bass
To rolling snares
Rhythm grabs you
Unawares

Vibrating your eardrums
Shaking the floors
Your mind is opened
To other doors

Lyrics can cut like a sword
They said the pen was mightier
They were not wrong

But, oh,
What of the melody?!
To forget that would be amiss!

Doom in the slowness
Walking you through the darkness
Through the tunnel
And the winding caves
Out and free on the other side

The song grabbed you
Gripped your hand
And took you away
But wow, it was worth it
You're back now
Fulfilled in the mind

Listen with me
Cry with me
Smile with me
Feel with me

Milton Keynes UK
Ingram Content Group UK Ltd.
UKHW042140281024
450365UK00001B/2